Making Spelling Words Stick!

50 FUN, TEACHER-TESTED IDEAS FOR ALL LEARNERS

by Richard S. Piccirilli and Todd A. Zuk

New York • Toronto • London • Auckland • Sydney
Mexico City • New Delhi • Hong Kong • Buenos Aires

Teaching *Resources*

DEDICATIONS

This work is dedicated to the memory of Carl. J. Diliberto,
a real nice guy who is dearly missed by all.
And to my wife, our children, and their families:
you are always in my thoughts. Love you all! RSP

To Mair, Ben, Brian, and Tucker—I love you. TAZ

ACKNOWLEDGMENTS

Not always seen, but always there, are my parents, my family, and my former teachers and students. To them a "thank you" for what they have taught me. Special thanks to Marianne Zuk for her literary skills and to my friend, colleague, and master teacher, Mike Quigley, for his comments and suggestions, and to Virginia Dooley for her encouragement. RSP

Thanks to Mair for her sharp eye. We couldn't do it without you. TAZ

Cover design by Maria Lilja
Edited by Wendy Vierow
Interior design by Solutions by Design, Inc.

ISBN 0-439-57626-1

2 3 4 5 6 7 8 9 10   40   11 10 09 08 07 06 05 04

Table of Contents

Introduction

As teachers, we are responsible for making sure our students become—and remain—good spellers. Therefore, our reason for writing this book is simple. It is to make this task fun, interesting, and relevant for students as well as for you, the teacher. This is achieved by presenting fifty practical, easy-to-use, and fun ideas. You may use your own spelling words and imitate the ideas explained in each spelling activity in your lesson plans.

The concept behind *Making Spelling Words Stick!* is best described by listing other titles we considered while writing this book:

* *Ideas to Brighten Up Your Spelling Lessons*
* *Fifty Ideas That Will Improve Pupil Achievement in Spelling*
* *Wake Up Your Spelling Program and Awaken Student Spelling Skills*
* *Activities for Your Weekly Spelling Words*
* *Spell Well, Well After the Spelling Test*
* *Fun With Your Weekly Spelling Words*
* *Models for Spelling Activities*
* *Using Your Spelling Skills in Writing*
* *Make Spelling Interesting and Relevant*
* *Teaching Spelling So That Students Will Remember What They Learned*

This book is about all the above and more. It is about having students care about correct spelling. It is about having students develop a *spelling conscience*—to care that the words they write are all correctly spelled.

A fact of life is that our written work, and therefore the worthiness of our ideas, is partly judged by correct spelling. Our knowledge, education, and integrity are also judged. Consequently, valuing correct spelling goes to the heart of creating better spellers.

Doing well on weekly spelling tests does not guarantee good spellers. Good spellers use correct spelling in their written work long after the weekly spelling tests. This is our challenge as teachers—to take our students beyond their spelling tests. To this end, this book can make a worthy contribution.

How This Book Is Organized

The spelling activities in this book can be used with any spelling list. We present models, but you can substitute your own spelling words. The models are flexible and suit any teaching situation. They have simple, clear directions. The word lists are used merely to demonstrate the learning activities. In some cases reproducibles are provided to simplify teacher duplication of the learning activity.

The spelling activities are grouped in sections that focus on one or more related aspects of spelling. These include:

Valuing Spelling—creating a class ethos to recognize and appreciate spelling's contribution to the clarity of ideas and its overall importance in communication. It is to help students realize that spelling is an essential school subject.

Developing Visual Memory—training to remember what one sees. This may involve examining words and visualizing the order of letters, the tall and short letters, and noting unique features in the word's appearance and shape. This may be especially useful to students who are visual learners.

Practice Using Spelling Words—opportunities to see, write, and develop an intuitive sense about the word. Practice is related to visual memory, word building, proofreading, and application. Practice also helps students personalize their spelling words.

Word Building—expanding spelling to different forms of a word. It can include defining the new word and learning to use it correctly, teaching word meaning as well as reinforcing phonics skills. Word building helps students realize they can spell many more words than just those they have studied.

Applying Spelling Words in Writing—using spelling skills on a regular basis. Using correct spelling in written work gives meaning and purpose to the study of spelling. It also demonstrates the diverse situations that require spelling skills.

Proofreading Spelling Words—finding spelling errors and correcting them without assistance. These activities point out the value of spelling and underscore the idea that proofreading requires patience and a discriminating eye.

These activities can be used in any order. Selection can be based on teacher and/or student interest and class need. This book is meant to be a flexible teacher tool.

Yes! Spelling Is Important

Purpose: Explain that correct spelling is important in life, that all livelihoods depend on correct spelling, and that there are consequences to incorrectly spelled words.

Materials: copy of page 8, scissors

What to Do: Cut a copy of page 8 along the dotted lines. Divide students into three groups. Give each group one scenario from page 8. Ask groups to discuss their scenario and to be prepared to talk about it to the class. Or if groups prefer, they can act out their scenarios for the class.

Use the situations below as a basis for further discussion. Invite appropriate adults who can attest to the following situations that emphasize the importance of correct spelling.

✳ A school principal or school secretary can tell about the care that is taken with school communications, such as school newsletters, reports to the superintendent, or notes to parents and teachers.

✳ A writer can tell why all written work needs to reflect correct spelling.

✳ An employer can tell what misspelled words on a job application say about the applicant.

✳ A signmaker can describe what happens when mistakes are made in his or her business.

✳ A newspaper reporter can tell why correct spelling is important to him or her.

✳ An editor can describe why correct spelling is important.

Spelling and You

Purpose: Reflect on the importance of correct spelling and its effect on daily life.

Materials: copies of page 9, paper, pencils or pens

What to Do: Distribute copies of page 9 to students and have them answer the questions. Invite them to share their answers with the class. As an alternative, you may wish to call on students for their answers.

Spelling Posters

Purpose: Students create posters to remind the class about the importance of spelling.

Materials: copies of pages 10–12, scissors, poster board or drawing paper, markers

What to Do: Copy pages 10–12, enlarging the pages if possible. Cut out the four posters on each page, and post all twelve around the classroom. Ask students to create a poster based on one of the models. As an alternative, use the models as a springboard, and ask students to create their own original spelling posters. Encourage students to decorate their posters.

Yes! Spelling Is Important

Your mother gives you a shopping list. She wants you to buy flour, but instead she writes f-l-o-w-e-r. What will happen when you get home? What will your mother say? What will you say?

You read a letter from a friend and a sentence in the letter contains these words: "My father bought me a new batt." What did you do when you came across the word "batt"? Did it make you stop? Did it stop the flow of the letter and what you were thinking? What is the problem with having to stop and figure out what is meant?

You are reading a classmate's story. What happens when you come to a misspelled word? What do you do? When you read someone else's work, does the writer have an obligation to the reader? Explain your answer.

Spelling and You

1. What happens when you read something that someone wrote and it has misspelled words in it? What does it tell you about the writer and his or her work?

_____

_____

2. List three jobs that depend on correct spelling.

_____

_____

3. What would happen if any of these jobs had products with misspelled words on them?

_____

_____

_____

4. How do you feel when someone misspells your name? What do you do about it? Why?

_____

_____

_____

5. Why do you think it is important to spell words correctly?

_____

_____

_____

6. Have you written something that made you think about correct spelling? What was it and when did you write it?

_____

_____

_____

Spelling Posters

Proper spelling is everyone's job!

Nothing says it better than spelling!

Spell check can't do it all!

A big BOO BOO is a misspelled word on a job application!

Making Spelling Words Stick! ✳ Scholastic Teaching Resources

Spelling Posters

To communicate in writing you need spelling!

Try writing without knowing how to spell correctly.

Where would you be without spelling?

A misspelling can result in a miscommunication!

Spelling Posters

Our class knows that correct spelling is important!

Did Alex find a poodle or a puddle?

Reading misspelled words can be annoying!

I know the difference among the words: they're, their, and there!

Making Spelling Words Stick! ❋ Scholastic Teaching Resources

Making Spelling Word Jumbles

Purpose: Strengthen visual memory by identifying words in spelling jumbles.

Materials: chalk, copies of page 14, pencils

What to Do: Use a copy of page 14 to create spelling word jumbles with your class spelling list. Use the samples below as a guide. After you have created your jumbles, copy your completed version of page 14 for students. Ask students to find and circle their spelling words. If you prefer, this activity may be done with an overhead or at the chalkboard, with students coming to the chalkboard to circle the words. You may also wish to provide students with blank copies of page 14 so that they can make their own jumbles for partners to solve.

Use cursive writing.

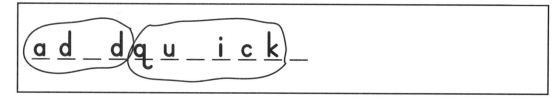

Separate words into smaller parts.

Separate words into smaller parts. Insert other letters in between the words.

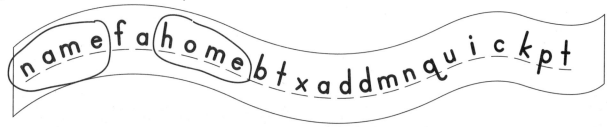

Spelling Word Jumbles

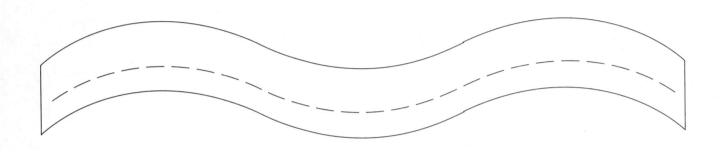

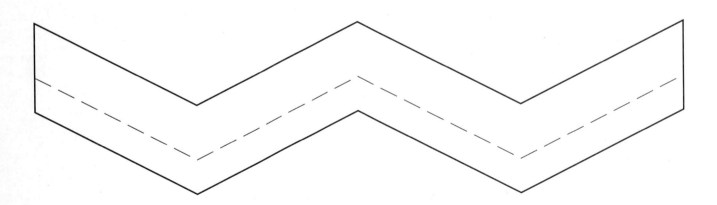

Making Spelling Words Stick! ☀ Scholastic Teaching Resources

Grid Spelling

Purpose: Develop visual memory by learning word configuration and details.

Materials: copies of page 16, pencils

What to Do: Reproduce the grid on page 16 as a transparency or make a quick grid drawing on the chalkboard. Model how to fill in the grid with spelling words. Write students' spelling words on the chalkboard. Distribute copies of page 16 to students. Have students fill in the grid starting with the spelling words that contain the fewest letters and working up to the words with the most letters. Ask students to alphabetize words that have the same number of letters.

Sample Spelling List
fair
fountain
automobile
garage
radio
radar

f	a	i	r						
r	a	d	a	r					
r	a	d	i	o					
g	a	r	a	g	e				
f	o	u	n	t	a	i	n		
a	u	t	o	m	o	b	i	l	e

Word Search

Purpose: Develop visual memory by performing word searches.

Materials: copies of page 16, pencils

What to Do: Create a grid on the chalkboard or use a copy of page 16 to create a transparency. Have volunteers come to the chalkboard or an overhead projector to fill in the grid with their spelling-list words. Words may be entered horizontally, vertically, diagonally, and backwards. Encourage students to have words intersect. After all the words have been included, have students fill in with extra letters. Continue this activity until you feel that students can make their own word searches. Then give each student a copy of page 16 to create word searches for a partner to solve.

Sample Spelling List
bike
project
ask
furniture
row
fault

f	u	r	n	i	t	u	r	e	k	s	a
	a		o					k			
		u		w				i			
			l					b			
				t							

Name _____   Date _____

Spelling Grid

Config Your Spelling Words

Purpose: Develop visual memory to remember the configuration of spelling words.

Materials: copies of page 18, pencils

What to Do: Write students' spelling list on the chalkboard. Point out the three basic configurations that form words. (See below.) Demonstrate how to make a configuration using a few spelling words. Ask students to decide which spelling word the configuration represents. It is possible that there is more than one right answer since a configuration can represent more than one word. Copy page 18 and distribute to students. Have partners make their own configurations of spelling words for each to guess.

Here are three basic **Configs**:

With these **Configs** you can **Config** any word.

Here is a **Config** for the word **"big."**

The examples below demonstrate what **Configs** are and how they can be used.

Note that a **Config** can represent more than one word.

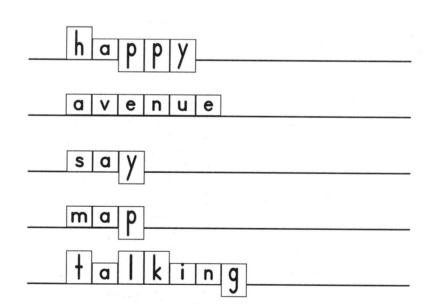

Sample Spelling List

talking

happy

map

say

avenue

Configs

In the left-hand column print spelling words. In the right-hand column make configurations of the spelling words. (See the sample.) Fold your paper along the dotted line. Give it to your partner so that the answers are hidden. The partner figures out what spelling word each config represents. Correct your partner's work by looking at the spelling words on the left-hand side.

Spelling Word	Config
spent	

Making Spelling Words Stick! ❄ Scholastic Teaching Resources

Can You Remember What You See?

Purpose: Improve visual memory skills through a memory game.

Materials: pencils, paper

What to Do: Provide students with pencils and paper. Tell them that you are going to give them a series of things to look at in order to test their memory. Follow these steps.

1. Make the following drawing on the chalkboard.

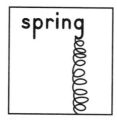

2. Direct them to study the drawing, noting the letters and anything unusual about it.

3. Ask students to close their eyes and try to see the drawing.

4. Cover the drawing and ask students to open their eyes and try to reproduce it.

5. After thirty seconds have passed (or whatever time you deem appropriate), uncover the drawing, and ask students to look at it.

6. Tell students that they can award themselves points on the following basis. Then ask students how many points they accumulated.

    1 point if all the letters are there.

    2 points if all the letters are in the right order.

    1 point if the word is printed.

    1 point if a box is made around the word.

    1 point if the letter "g" is extended to show a spring.

    1 point if the word is in the upper part of the square.

Create your own visuals for your class's spelling words. For each visual follow the same procedure used to remember the word *spring*. Below are more samples.

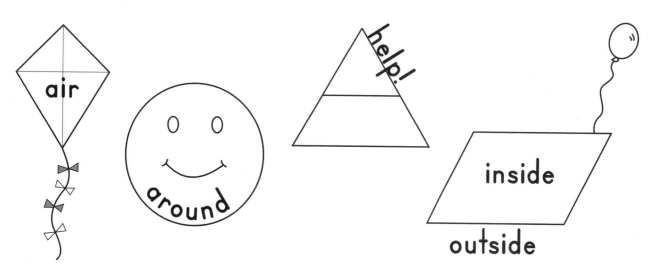

Lead into phrases and sentences using spelling words. For example:

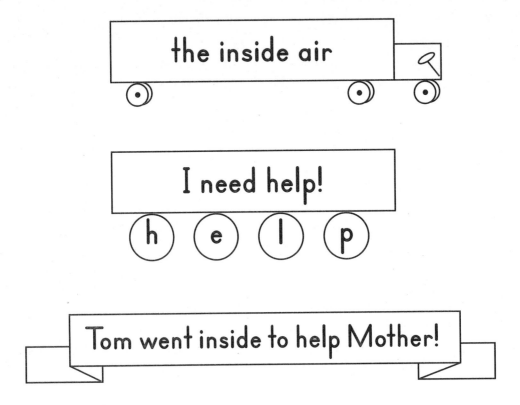

Total Recall

Purpose: Improve visual memory skills through word recall.

Materials: none

What to Do: Write three spelling-list words on the chalkboard. Give the class fifteen seconds to remember the words. Then, have them cover their eyes while you erase one of the three words. Ask a volunteer to write the missing word, spelling it correctly, on the chalkboard. As students develop a greater ability to remember what they see, cover up two words. Finally, cover up or erase three words and ask a volunteer to correctly spell the three missing words in their original order. Continue, expanding the list from three to five words.

Scrambled Spelling

Purpose: Provide close interaction with spelling words through visual memory, word configuration, ordering letters, and proofreading.

Materials: copies of page 22, markers or pencils, scissors, 3 x 5 index cards (optional)

What to Do: Write your spelling list on the chalkboard. Provide each student with two copies of page 22. Ask students to choose a word from a spelling list and spell it out by printing one letter in each box. For example, if the spelling word is **pencil** then a **p** is printed on one box, an **e** on another box, etc. Following the same procedure, ask students to fill up the remainder of page 22 with four other words from their spelling lists.

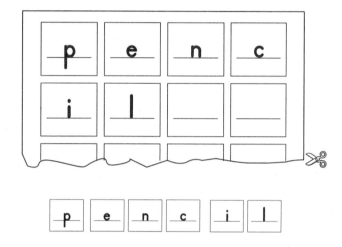

Have students cut out the boxes, being careful to keep each word in a separate pile. Direct students to perform the following activities:

✴ Take the letters from the first word and mix them up. Then put the letters in the correct order to spell the first word. Do the same for the remaining four words.

✴ Take all of the letters for all of the words and mix them up. Unscramble the letters to spell the five words.

✴ With a partner, exchange a scrambled word. Then unscramble each other's words. Continue with the remaining four words.

✴ Place all letters for one word in the correct order. Move one or more letters while a partner looks away. Ask the partner to guess which letter(s) were moved and then place the moved letter(s) in the correct order.

✴ Create new words by using some or all of the letters.

Instead of using copies of page 22, you may wish to have students write their letters on sturdy 3 x 5 index cards and play the activities above as a class at the chalkboard ledge.

Scrambled Spelling

Making Spelling Words Stick! ☀ Scholastic Teaching Resources

Missing Vowels

Purpose: Study spelling words to develop a visual image and understand sound-symbol relationships.

Materials: pencils, paper

What to Do: Below is a model for either a teacher-made worksheet or for group work at the chalkboard or the overhead. Students fill in the missing vowels for each of the spelling words. Another option is to allow students to make their own worksheets for other students to complete. If students are familiar with the spelling-word list, let them complete the exercise without viewing the list as they work.

Sample Spelling List

energy
judge
market
space
correcting
o'clock
television
each
forbid
bait

1. m_rk_t
2. t_l_v_s_ _n
3. b_ _t
4. c_rr_ct_ng
5. j_dg_
6. _ _ch
7. f_rb_d
8. _'cl_ck
9. _n_rgy
10. sp_ c_

Spelling in the Air

Purpose: Gain practice in visualizing spelling words through movement.

Materials: none

What to Do: Divide the class into two teams. With your back to the class, use your finger to write a spelling word in the air. Teams take turns identifying words, and then spelling them aloud correctly. Teams receive one point for each correct word identified and an additional point for each word spelled correctly. As a variation, have pairs of students take turns writing their own words in the air. Partners must guess the word.

Bowl of Fortune Spelling

Purpose: Improve visual memory of spelling-list words by playing a game based on the TV show *Wheel of Fortune.*

Materials: four copies of page 25, three copies of page 26, scissors, bowl

What to Do: Divide the class into three teams for this game, which lasts three rounds. Choose a different team to begin each round. The object of the game is to guess the missing letters in a word or phrase. Prepare a word or phrase made up of one or more spelling words. Draw squares on the chalkboard or on an overhead to represent each letter in the word or phrase. Make four copies of page 25, cut out the cards, and put them in a bowl. To begin play, a team member draws a slip of paper from the bowl. If the team member selects a money value, the team consults and chooses a letter that may be in the word or phrase. If the letter is correct, it is printed in the box or boxes in the proper locations, and students keep the money. If the team guesses correctly, it also gets to draw another card from the bowl and guesses another letter. Keep score by using a copy of page 26 for each team, writing down the money value for correct letters selected. The team that correctly guesses the spelling puzzle keeps the money earned during that round, while the losing teams do not. The winner is the team with the most money at the end of the three rounds.

Other Rules:

Vowels cost $200.

For **Bankrupt,** all winnings are forfeited.

A **Free Draw** cancels **Lose a Turn**.

Guessing the word or phrase can be done at any time.

A team's turn ends when it guesses a letter not in the word or phrase.

Bowl of Fortune Spelling Cards

Lose a Turn

Bankrupt

Free Spin

$100

$100

$100

$100

$500

$1,000

$5,000

Name _____   Date _____

Bowl of Fortune Letter List

Letter	Round 1 $Value $	Round 2 $Value$	Round 3 $Value$	Letter	Round 1 $Value $	Round 2 $Value$	Round 3 $Value$
A	_____	_____	_____	N	_____	_____	_____
B	_____	_____	_____	O	_____	_____	_____
C	_____	_____	_____	P	_____	_____	_____
D	_____	_____	_____	Q	_____	_____	_____
E	_____	_____	_____	R	_____	_____	_____
F	_____	_____	_____	S	_____	_____	_____
G	_____	_____	_____	T	_____	_____	_____
H	_____	_____	_____	U	_____	_____	_____
I	_____	_____	_____	V	_____	_____	_____
J	_____	_____	_____	W	_____	_____	_____
K	_____	_____	_____	X	_____	_____	_____
L	_____	_____	_____	Y	_____	_____	_____
M	_____	_____	_____	Z	_____	_____	_____
TOTAL	_____	_____	_____	TOTAL	_____	_____	_____

Making Spelling Words Stick! ❄ Scholastic Teaching Resources

Break the Code

Purpose: Scrutinize words to develop visual images by breaking a code.

Materials: copies of page 28, pencils

What to Do: Using a copy of page 28, create a Random Alphabet with all 26 letters in non-alphabetical order (see sample below). Write coded spelling words for your students to decipher in the Code Word column. Then copy the page again for students and distribute. To break the code, ask students to match the code letter from the spelling word in the Random Alphabet with its corresponding letter in the Regular Alphabet. Ask students to write the decoded word in the column marked Spelling Word. Another option is to have partners work together. Using copies of page 28, ask students to create a Random Alphabet and coded words and messages for their partners to decode.

Sample:

a	b	c	d	e	f	g	h	i	j	k	l	m	**Regular Alphabet**
e	a	j	q	h	o	t	n	v	s	d	z	l	**Random Alphabet**

n	o	p	q	r	s	t	u	v	w	x	y	z	**Regular Alphabet**
i	w	f	r	b	y	g	p	m	x	u	k	c	**Random Alphabet**

Sample Spelling List

history
neighbor
inn
computer
newspaper
knight
afternoon
arrive
stairs
sofa

1. vii = ___inn___
2. ywoe = ___sofa___
3. ygevby = ___stairs___
4. jwlfpghb = ___computer___
5. nvygwbk = ___history___
6. divtng = ___knight___
7. ihvtnawb = ___neighbor___
8. ihxyfefhb = ___newspaper___
9. eoghbiwwi = ___afternoon___
10. ebbvmh = ___arrive___

Break the Code

Create a Random Alphabet using 26 different letters. Write your spelling words in code under the heading that says Code Word. Then write a secret message and give this sheet to a partner to decode.

a	b	c	d	e	f	g	h	i	j	k	l	m	n	o	p	q	r	s	t	u	v	w	x	y	z

Code Word   ### Spelling Word

1. _____ = _____

2. _____ = _____

3. _____ = _____

4. _____ = _____

5. _____ = _____

6. _____ = _____

7. _____ = _____

8. _____ = _____

9. _____ = _____

10. _____ = _____

Secret Sentence: In the space below, write a coded message for a partner to decode.

_____

_____.

Spelling Break Time

Purpose: Become familiar with spelling words by recognizing and connecting the parts of words.

Materials: copies of page 30, pencils

What to Do: The object of this activity is for students to match the letters in Column A to those in Column B to create a spelling word. On a copy of page 30, write students' spelling words under the heading Spelling Words. In Column A, display beginning letters for each spelling word, mixing up the order of the words. In Column B, display the remaining letters of the word, again mixing up the order of the words. It is not necessary to break up a two-syllable word where it would normally divide. When you have finished breaking up each spelling word, make copies of the completed page for students to match.

Sample Spelling List

closet

secret

thinking

letters

another

fourteen

April

combination

teenage

however

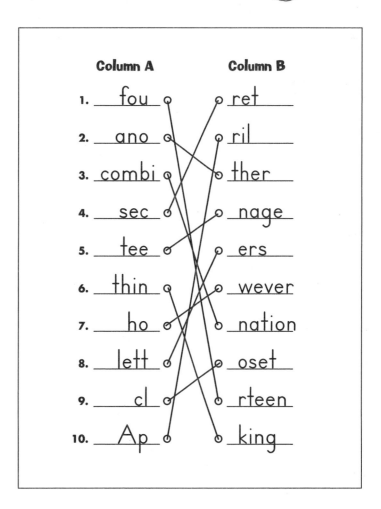

	Column A	Column B
1.	fou	ret
2.	ano	ril
3.	combi	ther
4.	sec	nage
5.	tee	ers
6.	thin	wever
7.	ho	nation
8.	lett	oset
9.	cl	rteen
10.	Ap	king

Spelling Breaks

Draw a line from the letters in Column A to the letters in Column B to create the spelling words shown.

Spelling Words	Column A	Column B
_____	1. _____ ○	○ _____
_____	2. _____ ○	○ _____
_____	3. _____ ○	○ _____
_____	4. _____ ○	○ _____
_____	5. _____ ○	○ _____
_____	6. _____ ○	○ _____
_____	7. _____ ○	○ _____
_____	8. _____ ○	○ _____
_____	9. _____ ○	○ _____
_____	10. _____ ○	○ _____

Making Spelling Words Stick! ☀ Scholastic Teaching Resources

Riddled With Spelling

Purpose: Become familiar with spelling words by creating riddles about them.

Materials: copies of page 32, pencils

What to Do: Distribute copies of page 32 to students. Write students' spelling words on the chalkboard. Ask students to create riddles from these words. Then have partners exchange papers to answer each other's riddles. Samples are shown below.

Sample Spelling List

history
quiet
station
island
page
onion
cart
ring
question
television

Riddle	Answer
I'm a circle.	1. ring
You can find trains here.	2. station
I'm a school subject.	3. history
I'm surrounded by water.	4. island
I'll bring tears to your eyes.	5. onion
I'm the opposite of noisy.	6. quiet
I ask something.	7. question
You use me when you shop.	8. cart
I'm found in a book.	9. page
Audiences watch me.	10. television

Acronym Spelling

Practice: Practice spelling words by creating acronyms.

Materials: paper, pencils

What to Do: For difficult spelling words, encourage students to make up acronyms. For example, if the difficult word is **debt,** students can make up sentences in which the first letter of each word spells the difficult word, such as "**D**ebbie **e**ats **b**uttered **t**oast." An example for the word **zany** is "**Z**oo **a**nimals **n**eed **y**ards." Allow students to share their acronyms with others.

Riddled With Spelling

Riddle   **Answer**

_____   1. _____

_____   2. _____

_____   3. _____

_____   4. _____

_____   5. _____

_____   6. _____

_____   7. _____

_____   8. _____

_____   9. _____

_____   10. _____

Making Spelling Words Stick! ☀ Scholastic Teaching Resources

An Extemporaneous Spelling Speech

Purpose: Reinforce spelling words by creating speeches about them.

Materials: none

What to Do: Explain to the class that an extemporaneous speech is one that is unplanned. The speaker is not quite sure of what he or she is going to say next and makes up the speech as he or she moves along. Use the samples for *pencil* and *lonesome* below to describe how to give an Extemporaneous Spelling Speech for the class. Then ask a volunteer to look at a spelling list word and tell as many different things as possible about the word. As a variation, play an Extemporaneous Spelling Speech game by dividing the class into teams. Award a team one point for each piece of information it gives about its word. The team with the most points wins.

The word is <u>pencil</u>.

* It has two syllables.

* It begins with a consonant.

* It ends with a consonant.

* It has six letters.

* It has two vowels.

* It has no long vowel sounds.

* It contains the word *pen*.

* You write with it.

* The *e* has a short vowel sound.

* It is a noun.

* You can make it plural by adding an *s*.

The word is <u>lonesome.</u>

* It is a compound word.

* It has two syllables.

* It has four consonants and four vowels.

* Both *e*'s are silent.

* The first *o* has a long vowel sound.

* Each consonant is followed by a vowel.

* It begins with a consonant.

* It has eight letters.

* It contains the words *one*, *so*, and *me*.

* It is a feeling.

Finger Spell Your Spelling Words

Purpose: Become familiar with spelling words by using the International Manual Alphabet.

Materials: copies of page 35

What to Do: Give each student a copy of page 35. Using the page as a reference, perform the following activities with students.

* ✳ Ask students to finger spell the letters *a, b,* and *d.* Then have volunteers come to the front of the room to demonstrate one of the three letters. Have the class guess the letter being finger spelled.

* ✳ Spell the following words and have students identify each: *bad, dad, dab, add, ad.*

* ✳ Introduce the letter *i* and finger spell the words *bid, did, aid,* and *bib.* An alternative is to write the four words on the chalkboard and have different students finger spell the words to the class.

* ✳ Choose spelling-list words that have the fewest letters and have the entire class finger spell them. Encourage students to look at the Manual Alphabet.

* ✳ Allow the class to practice the entire Manual Alphabet by finger spelling their own name, a friend's name, and the names of familiar objects.

* ✳ Have students finger spell their spelling words. This can also be done with partners or members of small groups who take turns finger spelling their spelling words for others to figure out.

* ✳ Have volunteers finger spell a spelling word while another volunteer writes out each letter on the chalkboard as each letter is being spelled.

* ✳ Have students test each other on their spelling words by giving each other a spelling word to finger spell.

Making Spelling Words Stick! ✳ Scholastic Teaching Resources

The International Manual Alphabet

A	B	C	D
E	F	G	H
I	J	K	L
M	N	O	P
Q	R	S	T
U	V	W	X
	Y	Z	

Slipping and Sliding

Purpose: Acquire spelling essentials by finding common elements in spelling-list words.

Materials: copies of page 38, scissors, pencils

What to Do: Write students' spelling words on the chalkboard or a transparency. Have students copy the spelling words on a copy of page 38. Another option is to print the words on a copy of page 38 yourself, and then distribute a copy of that page to students. Have students cut page 38 along the dotted lines. If students have filled in their own words on page 38, check to make sure they have copied them correctly by having partners compare slips. Alternatively, students may compare their slips with the words listed on the chalkboard or an overhead, or you may wish to have them check them as you recite the spelling of each word. Choose among the following activities for students.

✳ **Alphabetize**

Have students alphabetize the spelling words on their slips.

✳ **Vowels and Consonants**

Ask students to arrange spelling words into two groups of words: one beginning with vowels and the other with consonants. You may also wish to ask students to arrange the two groups alphabetically.

✳ **Letters**

Have students arrange spelling words in columns according to the number of letters in a word. Again, spelling words within each column can be alphabetized.

✳ **Syllables**

Ask students to arrange spelling words in columns according to the number of syllables.

✳ **Definitions**

Ask a question that includes a spelling word definition. For example, if one of the spelling words is *planet*, ask, "What am I? I am a heavenly body." Ask students to hold up the correct spelling word that answers the question.

✳ **Structure**

Ask a question about words that contain a silent letter, are plural, abbreviated, etc. Ask students to hold up the correct spelling word.

✳ **Password**

Ask students to hold up the spelling word that answers a clue you provided. For example, you might say "meal" in order to elicit the word "supper." Or, "not a dog, but a . . . " to elicit the word "cat." Pairs may also play the game, taking turns giving each other clues. You might also ask students to say the word and spell it for their answer.

Making Spelling Words Stick! ✳ Scholastic Teaching Resources

✳ **Pictionary**

Draw a picture on the chalkboard that is a clue to a spelling word. For example, you might draw a picture of the earth as a clue for the spelling word *planet*. Ask students to hold up the spelling word that goes best with the drawing and say the answer.

✳ **Charades**

Act out a spelling word. Students should hold up the slip showing the correct answer and say the answer. You may also wish to ask volunteers to act out words as well.

✳ **Concentration**

Ask partners to each contribute about 7–10 identical spelling words. Have them arrange the slips facedown in the shape of a rectangle. Pairs take turns turning over any two words, pronouncing words as they go. If the words match, that student keeps the match and wins another turn. If the spelling words do not match, then the slips are returned facedown. The winner is the student with the most matches.

Spelling Slip Maker

Which Word Is Which?

Purpose: Examine words and note various characteristics and structural details, such as configurations, sounds, sound-symbol relationships, letter sequences, prefixes, and suffixes.

Materials: copies of page 40, pencils

What to Do: On the chalkboard or an overhead, write students' spelling words and any of the following headings:

Plurals	Prefixes	Long Vowel Sounds
Nouns	Double Consonants	Long *a* or *e*, etc.
Suffixes	Double Vowels	One Syllable, Two, etc.
Compound Words	Silent Letter	Twin Vowels

Distribute a copy of page 40 to students. Ask students to copy the headings into the boxes on page 40. Direct students to arrange their spelling words under the correct headings. A sample is provided below.

Sample Spelling List
vehicle
hands
beets
airlines
happiness
softly
campgrounds
running

Plurals	**Nouns**	**Suffixes**
hands	hands	hands
campgrounds	campgrounds	beets
beets	happiness	airlines
airlines	vehicle	happiness
	beets	softly
		campgrounds
		running

Long *e*	**Twin Vowels**	**Compound Words**
vehicle	beets	airlines
beets		campgrounds

Which Word Is Which?

Valuable Words

Purpose: Combine spelling words with math.

Materials: copies of page 43, paper, pencils

What to Do: Before distributing page 43, tell students they will be using an alphabet chart to find the value of their spelling words. Demonstrate how to use an alphabet chart. Write the following on the chalkboard:

A	B	C	D	E	F	G	H	I	J	K	L	M	N	O	P	Q	R	S	T	U	V	W	X	Y	Z
1	2	3	4	5	6	7	8	9	10	11	12	13	14	15	16	17	18	19	20	21	22	23	24	25	26

Explain to students that each letter in the alphabet chart has a number value. Show students that with this value system, $b = 2$, $a = 1$, and $d = 4$, adding up to a total of 7 for the word *bad*. Practice examples using the chart on the chalkboard:

saw	19 + 1 + 23	=	43
happy	8 + 1 + 16 + 16 + 25	=	66
love	12 + 15 + 22 + 5	=	54
losing	12 + 15 + 19 + 9 + 14 + 7	=	76

Distribute a copy of page 43 to students. Dictate to students the number values that should go under each letter. Most students can work with the numbers 1-26, but you may wish to assign the repeated numbers of 1-5 for younger students or to match the level of the math class. You may also assign number values out of sequence—for example A = 14, B =21, etc. Ask partners to check each other's charts to make sure they are correct. Write students' spelling words on the chalkboard or an overhead. Choose from among the following activities for students to perform with their spelling charts.

* **Greatest and Least**

    Ask students to find the values of their spelling words. Have them determine the word with the greatest value and the word with the least value.

✴ 100 Chart

Ask students to find a word or words that have a value of 50 or 100. Keep a special chart for words with these values, adding to the chart as the class discovers in their lessons other words with a value of 100.

✴ Find the Word

Determine the values of each word ahead of time, and ask students to find the word with that value. For example, you might ask students to find a word with the value of 43. Ask students to share strategies for finding words quickly.

✴ Changing the Value

To help students develop strategies in determining word values, ask:

"How does adding an -s change a word's value?"

"How does adding an -ed change a word's value?"

"How can you tell which list words might have the greatest value?"

"Which letters seem to contribute to high values? to low values?"

Word Value Chart

A	B	C	D	E	F	G	H	I	J	K	L	M

N	O	P	Q	R	S	T	U	V	W	X	Y	Z

Making Spelling Words Stick! ✳ Scholastic Teaching Resources

Spelling Counts

Purpose: Become acquainted with spelling words by counting the number of letters in each word, recognizing the order of the letters, and using both critical thinking and trial and error strategies.

Materials: copies of pages 16 and 46, pencils

What to Do: Write the following sample spelling list on the chalkboard to demonstrate the activity for students.

Draw on the chalkboard the configuration below, with the letter *o* in the center square. Ask students to find two spelling words that fit in the squares. Point out that the *o*, where the two words intersect, is a clue. Ask students if there is more than one answer. *(possible answers down: gone, four; possible answers across: stool, flour, smoke).* Discuss with students how they arrived at their answers.

Sample Spelling List
gone
half
automobile
afternoon
four
knee
fee
got
stool
station
coffee
flower
cupboard
dresser
fortune
fraction
smoke

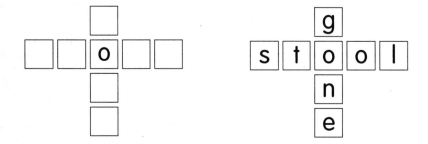

Draw on the chalkboard the configuration below, with the letter *f* as shown. Ask students to find words to fill into the squares. Have students discuss their strategies. Discuss with students why they have to do more than just count the number of letters in the words.

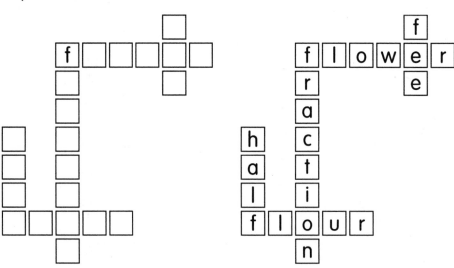

Making Spelling Words Stick! ✳ Scholastic Teaching Resources

Draw the crossword configuration shown below, placing the letters *o*, *t*, and *g* in the locations shown. Ask the class to find spelling words that fit into the squares.

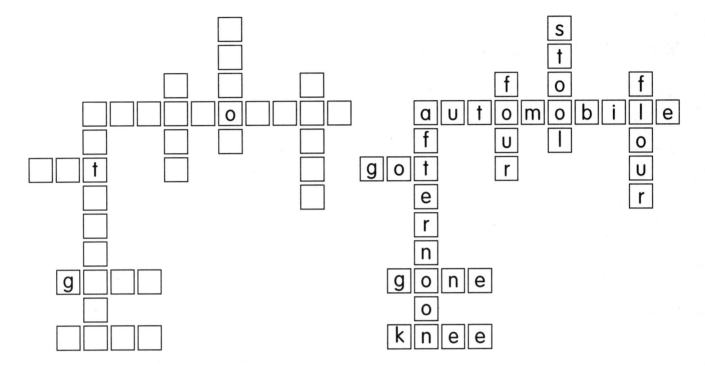

Using the grid on page 16, create your own configurations for your class's spelling words. It is best to start with the longest words, and then select shorter words to intersect with these words. Create squares by outlining selected squares with a dark pen, pencil, or marker. Then copy the page and distribute to students to complete. You may also wish to have students create their own configurations using a blank copy of page 16. Challenge students to create configurations that use all of their spelling words. In order to find words for configurations more quickly, students can use a copy of page 46 to organize their spelling words according to how many letters each word contains.

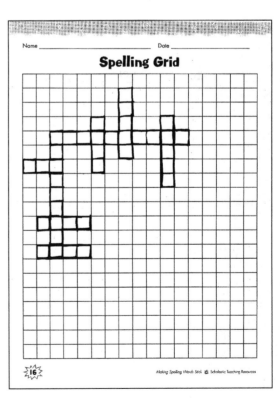

Spelling Counts

2-Letter Words	3-Letter Words	4-Letter Words	5-Letter Words
_____	_____	_____	_____
_____	_____	_____	_____
_____	_____	_____	_____
_____	_____	_____	_____

6-Letter Words	7-Letter Words	8-Letter Words	9-Letter Words
_____	_____	_____	_____
_____	_____	_____	_____
_____	_____	_____	_____
_____	_____	_____	_____

10-Letter Words	11-Letter Words	12-Letter Words	Other Words
_____	_____	_____	_____
_____	_____	_____	_____
_____	_____	_____	_____

Making Spelling Words Stick! ✻ Scholastic Teaching Resources

Spelling Lotto

Purpose: Practice spelling words and visualize letter sequences in the words.

Materials: copies of page 48, pencils

What to Do: Present letters in a grid, such as the one shown below, either on an overhead or the chalkboard. Using only those letters presented in the grid, model for students how to make as many spelling words as possible. You may repeat each letter more than once. You may wish to use the example below, pointing out that the words *mister, sister, due, just, pound, round,* and *garden* can be made from the letters in the grid.

Sample Spelling List

mister

due

pound

finger

garden

father

sister

pitcher

just

round

a	e	i	o	u	c
b	d	g	j	m	y
n	p	r	s	t	z

Distribute copies of page 48 to students. Dictate letters for students to fill into their grids. You may wish to make sure that the letters you dictate will result in the creation of some of your spelling words. List students' spelling words on the chalkboard, which they will copy into the left-hand column on page 48. Then ask students to sort the words into spelling-list words that can and cannot be made from the letters. Have them also list other words that can be made from the letters.

Spelling Lotto

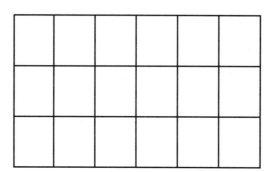

Spelling-List Words	Spelling Words That Can't Be Made	Spelling Words That Can Be Made	Other Words That Can Be Made
_____	_____	_____	_____
_____	_____	_____	_____
_____	_____	_____	_____
_____	_____	_____	_____
_____	_____	_____	_____
_____	_____	_____	_____
_____	_____	_____	_____
_____	_____	_____	_____
_____	_____	_____	_____
_____	_____	_____	_____

Making Spelling Words Stick! ✳ Scholastic Teaching Resources

Using Coordinates to Make Secret Codes

Purpose: Experience spelling-list words in a fun way by using a code made from coordinates.

Materials: copies of page 50, pencils

What to Do: The sample below shows a secret code box and coded words. Point out that the letters in the boxes are represented by coordinates made up of a letter and a number. The letters run along the side of the chart and the numbers run along the top of the chart. Show students how to find the coordinates of the first coded word. For example, in the sample below, the coordinates of the letter p are A2. Then demonstrate how to figure out the secret code for the first spelling word.

To make your own code for your class's spelling words, write the letters found in students' spelling words in the boxes on page 50. Guide students through the first example. In the column labeled "Spelling Words in Code" write the spelling words in code. Then copy and distribute to students. Have students decode their spelling words, then write a secret coded message to a partner. Ask partners to decode each other's messages.

Sample Spelling List
head
face
hands
teeth
feet
eyes
arms
neck
toes

	1	2	3	4	5	6	7	8	9
A	a	p	t	y	o	w	j	r	q
B	d	e	m	i	h	c	z	l	x
C	g	b	u	f	s	n	k	v	

B5, B2, A1, B1 (*head*)   C4, B2, B2, A3 (*feet*)

A3, A5, B2, C5 (*toes*)   B2, A4, B2, C5 (*eyes*)

A3, B2, B2, A3, B5 (*teeth*)   C4, A1, B6, B2 (*face*)

Secret Message:

B3, A4   C4, A5, A5, A3   B5, A1, C5   A1, C6   B4, A3, B6, B5.
(*My foot has an itch.*)

Using Coordinates to Break a Secret Code

	1	2	3	4	5	6	7	8	9
A									
B									
C									

Spelling Words in Code

_____

_____

_____

_____

_____

_____

_____

_____

Decoded Spelling Words

_____

_____

_____

_____

_____

_____

_____

_____

Write a secret message to a partner using your spelling-list words.

_____

_____

_____

_____

Spelling List Fill-Ins

Purpose: Gain practice using spelling words through storytelling.

Materials: transparency (optional)

What to Do: Prepare a story using as many spelling-list words as possible. Write the story (substituting numbered blank lines for spelling words) as a worksheet, on the chalkboard, or on a transparency. Ask students to number their papers, and use their spelling lists to fill in the blanks. Here is a sample:

My ____mother____ told me if I ____walked____
        1   2

a ____mile____ a day, I would ____become____
      3   4

healthier. After I ____tried____ it, I ____wrote____
                       5   6

to my grandfather and ____uncle____ and told them
                          7

that I was ____walking____ for ____exercise____.
               8   9

They wrote back to tell me that it was a good ____idea____.
                                                  10

> ### Sample Spelling List
> idea
> mile
> walking
> wrote
> exercise
> mother
> uncle
> walked
> tried
> become

G-u-e-s-s My Spelling Word

Purpose: See, spell, examine, and visualize spelling words through a simple game.

Materials: chalk, paper

What to Do: Write your spelling list on the chalkboard. Then, secretly write a spelling word on the chalkboard and cover the word with your hand or a piece of paper. Call on a volunteer who would like to guess the hidden word. Students can look at the spelling list to make guesses. Students must spell the word that they wish to guess, before pronouncing it. Following is an example of how the game might proceed for the hidden word *happiness*.

Teacher: Who would like to guess which spelling word I have hidden?

Student 1: Is the word c-h-a-i-r, *chair*? *(It is important that the student spell the word before it is said.)*

Teacher: C-h-a-i-r, *chair* is not the word. *(Again, it is important that the teacher spell the word before it is said.)*

Student 2: Is the word h-a-m-m-e-r, *hammer*?

Teacher: H-a-m-m-e-r, *hammer* is not the word.

Student 3: Is the word h-a-p-p-i-n-e-s-s, *happiness*?

Teacher: H-a-p-p-i-n-e-s-s, *happiness* is the word. You may now come to the chalkboard and write your spelling word to hide for others to g-u-e-s-s.

The game continues in the same manner.

> ### Sample Spelling List
> bump
> prime
> chair
> inspire
> happiness
> feast
> earth
> hammer

Picturing Plural Spelling Words

Purpose: Make singular and plural spelling words more meaningful through art.

Materials: paper, pencils, colored markers

What to Do: Have students identify spelling-list words that are nouns and name the plural for each. Ask students to draw pictures for both the singular and plural form. Students may wish to color their drawings. As a variation, you can make drawing(s) of singular or plural nouns and ask students to come to the chalkboard and spell the word correctly. Or you might ask students to write a separate sentence for both the singular and plural forms of their spelling words.

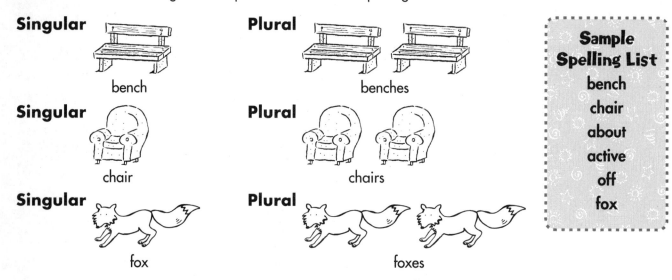

Singular   bench   **Plural**   benches

Singular   chair   **Plural**   chairs

Singular   fox   **Plural**   foxes

Sample Spelling List
bench
chair
about
active
off
fox

Finding Hidden Little Words

Purpose: Aid word building and focus on letters that comprise a spelling word.

Materials: copies of page 53, pencils

What to Do: Write students' spelling-list words on the chalkboard. Distribute copies of page 53 to students. Ask students to write their spelling words in the boxes. Then ask them to find hidden smaller words within their spelling words (see sample below). Tell students that they may not rearrange letters in order to create new words. Explain that some words may not contain any hidden words. As a variation, say a hidden word that comes from one of the spelling-list words. Ask students to guess the spelling list word from which it came. Another variation is to have students make other words using non-sequential letters.

season			little
sea	on	as	lit
seas	so	son	it
a			I

mister		visit	
mist		I	sit
is		is	
I		it	

afternoon		paper	
after	on	pa	per
noon	tern	a	
no	aft	pap	

Sample Spelling List
season
little
mister
visit
paper
door
afternoon
table

Making Spelling Words Stick! ✳ Scholastic Teaching Resources

Finding Hidden Little Words

Write your spelling words in the boxes. Next, find hidden little words in your spelling words. Write as many little words as you can find on the lines below each box.

Fix With a Prefix

Purpose: Create other word forms by adding selected prefixes to spelling words.

Materials: paper, pencils

What to Do: Write prefixes on the chalkboard or the overhead that would work well with your spelling words. Then write your spelling list on the chalkboard. Tell students that they will use the prefixes to create new word forms from the spelling word list (see sample below). Explain that some words may not work with prefixes, while others may work with more than one prefix. Call on volunteers to add prefixes to the spelling words. Or you may wish to have students work independently at their desks, creating a list of new words with paper and pencil. After students have mastered prefixes, you may wish to play a similar game with suffixes.

cook	like	able	arrange
precook	dislike	unable	rearrange
recook			

Sample Spelling List

food
cook
kitchen
heat
like
onion
pay
kettle
believe
able
soup
arrange
agree
taste

Presto Change-o

Purpose: Focus on spelling words and expand spelling skills to other related words.

Materials: pencils, paper

What to Do: Have students select a spelling word and change something about the word to create a new word. Have students share their Presto Change-o words at the chalkboard or at the overhead projector. Ask the class to figure out how each word was made from the previous word. Use the examples below to demonstrate how to create a Presto Change-o.

Sample Spelling List

folder
nest
not
sit
happy

folder	folder older holder colder bolder boulder
nest	nest best test tested vested rested arrested
not	not no nothing something someone somewhere
sit	sit sat fat fan tan tin bin win won son
happy	happy snappy snap nap nape cape tape

Making Spelling Words Stick! ✹ Scholastic Teaching Resources

Spelling Crossword Puzzle

Purpose: Use spelling words in the context of a crossword puzzle to build vocabulary, recognize letter order, and understand how a word is spelled.

Materials: copies of page 16, pencils

What to Do: Use the grid paper on page 16 for building a crossword puzzle using your spelling-word list. See the sample below. (If you prefer, computer programs are available to prepare crossword puzzles.) Then copy your completed crossword and distribute it to students. You may wish to have students work alone or in pairs to complete the puzzle.

Sample Spelling List

- frost
- noun
- hope
- trust
- run
- snow
- notes
- page
- often

ACROSS

1. Regularly
4. Frosty likes it
6. Antonym for distrust
8. In a book
9. Person, place, or thing

DOWN

2. Jack _____
3. Messages
4. Odd number
5. Faith, _____, charity
7. Exercise

Word Building

Purpose: Increase spelling skills by building on root words through the use of prefixes, suffixes, and compounds.

Materials: paper, pencils, dictionaries (optional)

What to Do: Tell students they will be using their spelling words as a base from which to build other words using prefixes, suffixes, and compounds (see sample below). Choose words from your spelling list that are appropriate for this activity. Write the words on the chalkboard. Ask students to write all of the word forms that can be made from the chosen words. You may choose to have students work together as a class, in small groups, with partners, or individually. Students may add prefixes, suffixes, or other words to create open or closed compound words. You may wish to provide students with dictionaries. As an extension, have small groups create posters of word-building possibilities for different spelling words, and post them around the classroom.

You may wish to ask volunteers to identify the word parts in each example.

Sample Spelling List
work
finger
agree
help
gather
walk
mother

work

works	working
worked	worker
workers	workhorse
workhorses	workhouse
workhouses	workaholic
workaholics	waterworks
housework	

finger

fingers	fingered
fingering	fingernail
fingernails	fingering
fingerprint	fingerprints
fingerprinted	fingerprinter
fingertip	fingertips

agree

agree	agrees
agreed	agreeing
agreement	agreements
agreeable	agreeably
disagree	disagrees
disagreed	disagreeing
disagreement	disagreements
disagreeable	

help

helps	helper
helpers	helped
helpings	
helping hand	

Spelling Thesaurus

Purpose: Reinforce the spelling and meaning of spelling-list words through the use of synonyms.

Materials: thesaurus, paper, pencils, poster paper, colored markers

What to Do: Write students' spelling words on the chalkboard. Tell students that they are going to find synonyms for their spelling words (see sample below). Provide small groups of students with a thesaurus. Have groups use it to find synonyms for their spelling words. Students should jot down the synonyms on a piece of paper. Next, give each group poster paper and colored marking pens. Have groups transfer their researched words to the poster. Encourage students to decorate their posters. Hang students' posters around the room for reference and display. As a variation, have students perform the same activity by finding antonyms for their spelling words.

Sample Spelling List

walk
large
cheerful
student
around
job
take
sad

job

task
work
chore
employment
trade
profession
occupation
business
assignment

take

nab
capture
nip
confiscate
grip
seize
hook
wrench
carry off

sad

dismal
dejected
downbeat
mournful
sorrowful
mirthless
joyless
upset
crestfallen

large

sizeable
vast
immense
monstrous
mammoth
huge
gigantic
enormous
oversize

Describing Your Spelling Words

Purpose: Build relationships with spelling-list words by enhancing their meaning with descriptive words.

Materials: copy of page 59, pencils

Sample Spelling List

automobile

eating

children

drive

lunch

skip

shoes

handkerchief

What to Do: Write students' spelling words on the chalkboard or an overhead. Ask volunteers to identify nouns in the list. Or you may wish to have students raise their hands to identify nouns as you read the entire list aloud. Have students list the nouns under the heading Nouns on the copy of page 59. You may wish to tell the class the number of nouns in the spelling list to help them find all the nouns. Then, ask students to write an adjective that describes the noun under the heading Adjective. See the sample below. Make them repeat the activity for Verbs and Adverbs.

Adjectives	Nouns
fancy	automobiles
delightful	children
large	lunch
pointy	shoes
lacy	handkerchief

Getting to the Root of It

Purpose: Focus on spelling review words and expand spelling skills to other word forms.

Materials: paper, pencils

What to Do: Write spelling words which employ prefixes and suffixes on the chalkboard, an overhead, or on a worksheet for student use. Ask students to identify the root word aloud or in writing. Remind students that some root words undergo spelling changes when suffixes are added.

1. the youngest brother _____ young _____

2. to rename a boat _____ name _____

3. a couple of older people _____ old _____

4. an unhappy customer _____ happy _____

5. the twin babies _____ baby _____

6. a previewed video _____ view _____

7. a healthy appetite _____ health _____

8. remembering an anniversary _____ remember _____

9. to disrespect someone _____ respect _____

10. a friendly disagreement _____ agree _____

Describing Your Spelling Words

List your spelling words.

_____   _____

_____   _____

_____   _____

_____   _____

_____   _____

Now list the nouns and verbs in the correct columns. Then fill in adjectives and adverbs.

Adjectives	**Nouns**	**Verbs**	**Adverbs**
_____	_____	_____	_____
_____	_____	_____	_____
_____	_____	_____	_____
_____	_____	_____	_____
_____	_____	_____	_____
_____	_____	_____	_____
_____	_____	_____	_____
_____	_____	_____	_____
_____	_____	_____	_____

Graffiti Board

Purpose: Become familiar with spelling words by creating graffiti.

Materials: bulletin board paper, colored markers

What to Do: Write students' spelling words on the chalkboard. Cover the bulletin board with paper and label it *Graffiti Board*. Provide students with colored markers. Ask students to write a sentence, which includes one of their spelling words, on the **Graffiti Board**. Have students underline their spelling words. Encourage students to draw a cloud, circle, square, diamond, or some other shape around their sentences.

Sample Spelling List

stove

gas

tie

fourth

excellent

biting

smoke

dime

group

piece

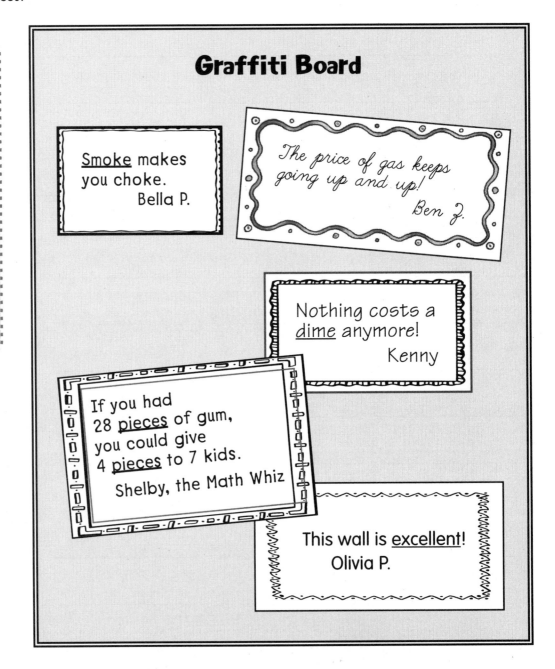

Graffiti Board

Smoke makes you choke.
Bella P.

The price of gas keeps going up and up!
Ben Z.

Nothing costs a dime anymore!
Kenny

If you had 28 pieces of gum, you could give 4 pieces to 7 kids.
Shelby, the Math Whiz

This wall is excellent!
Olivia P.

Funny Titles and Authors

Purpose: Use spelling-list words in the titles of books and/or names of authors.

Materials: copies of page 62, colored markers

What to Do: Model how to create a silly title or author's name using a spelling word from your class list, as shown below. To warm up the class, you may wish to have students fill in a missing spelling word in silly titles or authors' names that you have created. You may choose to have students work individually, in pairs, or in teams. Distribute copies of page 62 to students. Ask them to create funny titles and author names that incorporate their spelling words. Encourage students to decorate their book covers and highlight the spelling words. Allow students to share their humorous book titles and authors with the class.

Sample Spelling List

million
hurt
broken
pain
glass
easy
wise

How to Make a
Million Dollars
By
Penny Wise

Addition
Made Easy
By
Adams Up

Broken Mirror

By
Chip A. Glass

Pain in the Neck

By
T. Hurt

Funny Titles and Authors

By

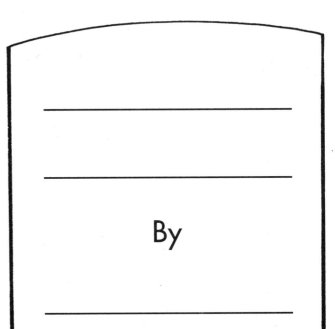

By

By

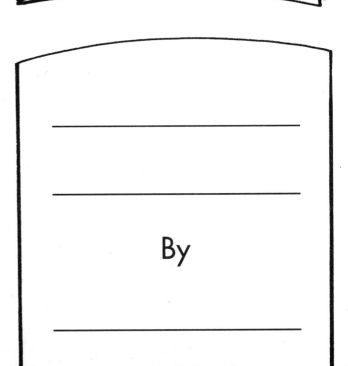

By

Making Spelling Words Stick! ✳ Scholastic Teaching Resources

Tricky Tongue Twisters

Purpose: Use spelling words in tongue twisters.

Materials: pencils, paper, poster board, colored markers

What to Do: Demonstrate a tongue twister, using students' past or present spelling lists and write it on the chalkboard. Below are examples with a sample spelling list. Tell students they will write a tongue twister using words from one of their spelling lists. Direct them to use two or more spelling words that begin with the same sound to create their tongue twisters. Be sure to provide opportunities for students to share their tongue twisters with the class. You may wish to allow students to create *Tricky Tongue Twisters* posters for classroom display. Encourage students to illustrate their posters.

The _kind_ _King_ of Keypin kept a key with his kin, Kim of Kimberly.

The beautiful black _basket_ was bought by Betty Beagle at Barney's _Basement_.

The slippery _silver_ snake sent by Mr. Silas Silverman sat on the shiny _stone_.

Frannie's Fancy Flower Shop _forbids_ friendly customers to fiddle with its _fresh_ flowers.

The _hardworking_ _horse_, Henry, headed toward the hay after giving a helping hand to farmer Harvey Hillhouse.

Sample Spelling List
candle
kind
basement
fresh
dare
silver
closet
basket
hardworking
money
king
forbid
engine
horse
stone

Sentence Expansions

Purpose: Use newly learned words.

Materials: pencils, paper

What to Do: Provide a basic sentence using your spelling-list words. Have students expand the sentence with adjectives, adverbs, and other parts of speech. Ask them to add information such as who, when, where, how, and why. Direct students to underline their spelling words in their sentences. Following is a sample spelling list and examples.

Sample Spelling List
enjoys
planted
furniture
inform
night
ocean

Shewana _enjoys_ shopping.

My cousin, Shewana, definitely _enjoys_ shopping in the more expensive stores at the Penfield Mall.

Mohammed _planted_ seeds.

Mohammed arranged for the newly _planted_ seeds to be watered daily by his Aunt Nasha.

The _furniture_ is new.

The family room _furniture_ is new and was recently purchased at Kelly's Furniture Store at the corner of State Street and Skyline Drive in Cape Coral, Florida.

Rhyme Time Spelling

Purpose: Apply spelling skills by writing rhyming sentences.

Materials: pencils, papers, colored markers

What to Do: Direct students to make rhyming sentences based on a chosen spelling list word. You may wish to provide students with an opening line. Below are some examples. After students have created their rhymes, ask them to write them on a piece of paper and illustrate their rhymes. You may wish to display students' rhymes around the classroom.

Our class was **glad**
That they were sung to by a lad
Who stood on a pad.

You need to boil **oil**
And not toil with soil.

There were **nine**
Vines to make wine.
But the fine wine
Was all mine.

Sample Spelling List

glad

fish

oil

nine

mix

test

teach

cable

motion

To expand students' ability to spell other words, use weekly spelling words as a basis to make rhyming words. The rhyming words can be made into charts and hung in the classroom. Below are some examples from the sample spelling list.

mix
fix, nix

test
vest, pest, jest, nest, chest, zest, rest, best

teach
preach, reach, beach

cable
fable, table, able, stable, sable

motion
notion, lotion, potion

Newspaper Ads

Purpose: Practice spelling-list words and reinforce the idea that correct spelling is important and relates to the real world.

Materials: pens, pencils, paper

What to Do: Have students write a newspaper ad using words from their spelling list. Ask students to underline their spelling words. Explain to students that different forms of the word are permitted.

Sample Spelling List

round
eyes
enjoys
morning
promises
homework
dear
please
didn't
number
wait
looking
students
school
factory
cottage
included

For Sale: Dog named Tucker. He has large <u>round</u> <u>eyes</u> and is friendly. He <u>enjoys</u> a <u>morning</u> nap. He <u>promises</u> not to eat your math <u>homework</u>. Call: Carol at 281-BOOK.

Personals: My <u>dear</u> sister, Tina. <u>Please</u> call me at 377-3897. Sorry I <u>didn't</u> get your new phone <u>number</u>. Can't <u>wait</u> to see you at the family dinner. Love, your brother, Tim.

Help Wanted: H. M. Page Company <u>looking </u>for bright <u>students</u> to work after <u>school</u> in book <u>factory</u>. Excellent pay. Call: 243-1010.

For Rent: Consensus Lake. Cottage sleeps 8. Boat <u>included</u>. $550 per week. Call: Richard at 243-4788.

Spelling Poetry

Purpose: Use spelling-list words in a novel and meaningful way by creating poetry.

Materials: pencils, paper

What to Do: Ask students to choose a spelling-list word as a basis for creating a short poem. Explain that each letter of the spelling word will be the first letter in the first word in each line of poetry. Students may choose to make their poems rhyme or not. Have students create illustrated posters of their poems to hang around the classroom. See the examples below.

Sample Spelling List

almost

pay

inch

ask

window

rocker

thumb

wrist

phone

file

ALMOST
Ann Arnold makes cookies that
Lucy just loves.
Molasses and
Oatmeal are great, but
Sweet chocolate chips
Taste the best!

PAY
Pedro and Maria
Arrived from Mexico
Yesterday morning.

INCH
Inside the tower of
North
Church there
Hides a bell.

ASK
As soon as Sam saw the light,
Sam thought that it was too bright, so he
Kept his eyes shut and missed the sight.

As a variation, have students use each letter of their spelling word to write spelling words from previous lessons.

almost
answer
late
mister
ocean
shore
toys

Spotting Spelling Errors

Purpose: Develop proofreading skills.

Materials: paper, pencils

What to Do: Present sentences with the week's words for proofreading. This activity may be used as a chalkboard, overhead, or worksheet lesson. When writing sentences, indicate how many errors are present by using parentheses at the end of each sentence. You may also wish to have students proofread with a list of their spelling words in front of them. Discuss with students how well they can spot spelling errors. Sample sentences are shown below.

Sample Spelling List
tired
village
music
grows
spare
steam
festival

1. Ken Fu ~~groes~~ grows flowers in his ~~spar~~ spare time. (2)

2. Tulana enjoys singing happy ~~musik~~ music. (1)

3. There was ~~stream~~ steam coming from the boiling pot. (1)

4. The ~~villege~~ village people had a ~~festivel~~ festival. (2)

5. The campers were ~~tried~~ tired and hungry. (1)

Hunting for Misspellings

Purpose: Find misspelled words to improve proofreading skills.

Materials: copies of paragraphs with errors, paper, pencils

What to Do: Collect samples of students' writing that contain spelling errors. You may wish to use the work of your own students or, to maintain privacy, work belonging to another class. Or you may choose to write samples yourself that contain misspelled spelling-list words for students to proofread. If possible, select paragraphs with cursive writing, since it tends to reflect how students will actually see written work that needs proofreading. If you wish, you may indicate the number of errors in parentheses after each paragraph. Copy the paragraphs and distribute to students. Ask students to circle the misspelled words, then spell them correctly on another piece of paper. Below are two sample paragraphs.

Our Neighbor Mrs. Pelot

When our puppy, Josifa, (whent) into Mrs. Pelot's (gardan,) Mrs. Pelot didn't lose her temper. Josifa had (dugg) a big (whole) in her (flour) beds. Mrs. Pelot had (ben) working on them all afternoon. (6)
Mrs. Pelot called Josifa to come to her. Then she gave Josifa a (tret.) (She's) a (vary) kind neighbor. (2)

went
garden
dug
hole
flower
been
treat
very

February 14, 2004

(Deer) Grandma Sylvia, (1)
I loved the postcard you sent from Italy. The picture of the (curch) looks like the one in our (towne) (2)
I also want to thank you for my birthday (gifte) It was (thoughtfull) of you. (2)
It will be fun when (your) here this summer staying with us for a (weak.) (2)
Thanks (againe) for the card. (1)
Love,
Morgan

dear
church
town
gift
thoughtful
you're
week
again

Proofreading Newspaper Ads

Purpose: Proofread and appreciate the value of correct spelling in written communication.

Materials: copies of newspaper ads with errors, pencils, paper

What to Do: Prepare copies of newspaper ads made up of spelling word errors. You may wish to use the ads students made up from a previous lesson (see Newspaper Ads, page 65). Before copying ads, you may wish to include lines after each ad on which students can write corrected words. You may also wish to indicate in parentheses the number of errors that students must find in each ad. Make copies of the ads and distribute to students. Have students place an "X" on any misspelled word and write the correct spelling word in the spaces below the ad or on a piece of paper. Below are samples on which you can base your worksheet for students.

Sample Spelling List
cheap
bee
only
sale
left
new
summer
box
one
almost

For Sail: Be's honey. Fresh. Onle $.75/pint. Call 243-4766.

sale

bees

only

For Sale: Doris Doll in original boxe. Only won lefte. $25. Call Tiegan at 281-DOLL.

box

one

left

For Sale: Office Furniture. 2 chairs, 2 desks. Cheep. Call Bob at 697-6110.

cheap

_____

_____

For Sale: Summer clothing. Almosst knew. Garage Sale. 5317 West Lake Road

almost

new

_____

Detective Work: Find the Misspelled Word

Purpose: Practice proofreading.

Materials: paper, pencils

What to Do: Write four spelling-list words with one word misspelled in each group on the chalkboard, an overhead projector, or on a worksheet for students. Include a space to the right of each entry in which students can write corrected versions of the misspelled words. You may also include entries in which all four words in a group are spelled correctly. Consider using review words for this activity. If you wish, provide students with their spelling lists for proofreading. Ask students to circle the spelling word in each group that is misspelled. Then, in the space at the right, have them write the correct spelling. If all of the words in each group are spelled correctly, direct students to write "OK" in the space. Below are sample entries.

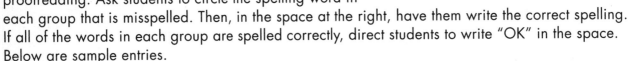

Sample Spelling List

art
special
got
stop
stick
suppose
again
compute
notice
gum
own
flight

1. stick   stoop   stop   (specail)   special

2. over   (knotice)   flight   gum   notice

3. got   guess   art   average   OK

4. own   rubber   (supose)   yet   suppose

5. (againe)   fun   picture   compute   again

Be a Dictator!

Purpose: Develop proofreading skills by listening, writing down, and proofreading dictated sentences.

Materials: paper, pencils

What to Do: Here is a way to help students be more attentive as they write and to take pride in what they are doing. Following are procedures for dictating as well as a suggested lesson plan to introduce the dictation procedure. Be sure to create sentences that are grade-level appropriate. You may wish to use student names in your sentences. Some students may find it helpful if you tell them how many words are in each dictated sentence. Students should be prepared to take dictation with paper and pencil.

Dictation Procedures

The general plan is:

* Students proceed only as they are told to do so.

* Each dictated sentence will be read aloud three times.

* Students repeat the sentence aloud.

* Students have two opportunities to proofread their sentences by pointing to each word with their pencils. Keep the sentences short to medium in length.

Teacher: We are going to learn how to do dictation. You will find it different, interesting, useful, and fun. I will read a sentence to you only three times during this activity, so you will have to be a good listener. Are you ready?

Students: Yes!

Teacher: Here's how it works. First, listen as I read a sentence aloud. Next, when I tell you to, repeat the sentence aloud. Finally, when I tell you to, begin writing the sentence. Let's begin. Here is the first sentence for the first time. The sentence is **Jane rode her new bike to school today.** Now, repeat the sentence aloud.

Students: Jane rode her new bike to school today.

Teacher: OK. You may now write the sentence.

(Students should be writing the sentence that they just said aloud. Allow enough time for everyone to finish.)

Teacher: I notice that everyone is finished writing. Now, I will read you the same sentence again. Take your pencil and put it under each word in the sentence as I say it. If you find any mistakes you want to correct, go ahead and correct them after I have finished reading the sentence. You may find that you put in an extra word that wasn't dictated or left out a word, or you did not spell a word correctly. Have your pencils ready to point to each word. Here is the sentence for the second time. I will read it very, very slowly: **Jane - rode - her - new - bike - to - school - today.**

(Students should be following along by pointing to each word as you slowly read the sentence.)

Teacher: Make any necessary corrections. You seem to be getting the hang of it quite well. I will read the sentence aloud for the third and final time in a little while. In the meantime, let's try this again with another sentence. Here is the new sentence. Be ready to repeat the sentence only when I tell you to. And remember to write the sentence only after I give you the signal. Here we go. Here is the sentence: **Did you find Tim's lost lunch?** All right, everyone repeat the sentence to me.

Students: Did you find Tim's lost lunch?

Teacher: Good, now you may write the sentence.

(Students should be writing the sentence you just dictated. Allow enough time to finish.)

Teacher: I notice you're finished. Now, I will read the same sentence again. Have your pencils ready to point to each word. Here we go. I will read the sentence very, very slowly: **Did - you - find - Tim's - lost - lunch?** Fix your sentence as you need to.

(Students should be following along by pointing to each word as you slowly read the sentence, and making the needed corrections. Continue with this dictation procedure until all of the sentences have been given.)

Teacher: Now, class, I will repeat all the sentences for the last time. It will be your last opportunity to make sure your sentences are correct. Point with your pencils as you did before. Make any last-minute corrections that you need to make. Ready? Here we go. Point and make your corrections. The first sentence was, **Jane rode her new bike to school today.** (*Pause.*) Point and make your corrections. (*Continue repeating for all the sentences.*) The last sentence was, **Did you find Tim's lost lunch?**

Write the dictated sentences on the chalkboard. Ask the pupils to compare their sentences with the chalkboard sentences for accuracy. Direct students to put a check mark in front of each sentence that matches perfectly. Collect papers and write comments on each paper such as: "Good job! Nice listening! You got most of it correct. Good!" You may wish to create a classroom display of student sentences titled "Our Very Best Work."

You may wish to assign credit value to each sentence. Inform students of the point value ahead of time so that students can focus on the credited elements. The criteria for assigning point value are flexible. For example, the first sample sentence, "Jane rode her new bike to school today," may have a value of eight points as follows: one point is earned if all the words are there; one point is earned if the sentence begins with a capital letter; one point is earned if the sentence ends with the proper mark of punctuation; one point is earned for neatness or cursive writing; one point is earned for each of the major words spelled correctly. (In the sample case, 'rode', 'bike', 'school', and 'today' are the major words.) You may wish to record students' points in your grading book.

Different sentences may present different opportunities to earn points. These may include points for an apostrophe, a hyphen, a hyphenated word, and other punctuation.

Spelling Portfolios Made Easy

Purpose: Make folders for monitoring spelling progress.

Materials: manila folders, copies of page 75, copies of page 76, stapler, colored pencils and markers

What to Do: Using spelling folders will encourage better spelling by helping students monitor and record their spelling progress. Spelling folders allow students to track missed words that they need to spell correctly. The basic premise is that when students become more fully aware of their progress, it will motivate them to maintain high standards of spelling.

✸ Have students use a manila folder and markers to design a cover for their spelling folders using a spelling theme. For example, a cover might include letters, prefixes, or other elements of spelling.

✸ Next, ask students to construct a bar graph using a copy of page 75. As students complete final tests throughout the year, have them record their spelling scores on the graph with colored markers. Have students staple the graph to the inside of their spelling folder.

✸ Have students store their final spelling tests in their spelling folder.

✸ Have students create a Personal Spelling List, using a copy of page 76. Students can use this list to correctly write spelling words that they missed on final tests. The list could also contain corrected words from students' written work such as review tests, book reports, creative writing, and other projects. Ask students to staple their lists to the inside of the folder.

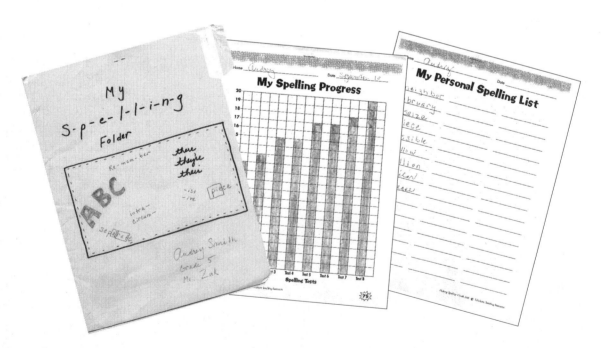

Making Spelling Words Stick! ✸ Scholastic Teaching Resources

Name _____   Date _____

My Spelling Progress

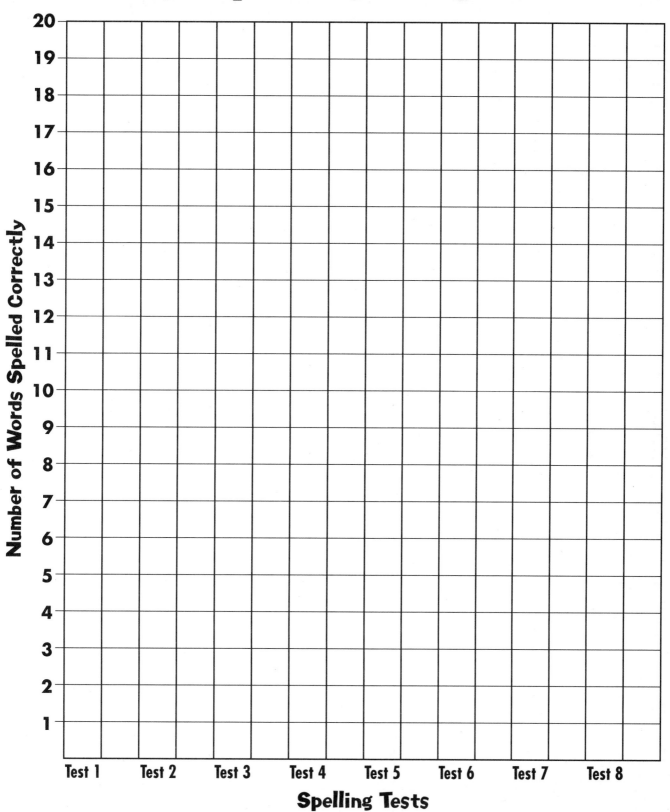

Number of Words Spelled Correctly

20
19
18
17
16
15
14
13
12
11
10
9
8
7
6
5
4
3
2
1

Test 1   Test 2   Test 3   Test 4   Test 5   Test 6   Test 7   Test 8

Spelling Tests

Name _____ Date _____

My Personal Spelling List

_____ _____ _____

_____ _____ _____

_____ _____ _____

_____ _____ _____

_____ _____ _____

_____ _____ _____

_____ _____ _____

_____ _____ _____

_____ _____ _____

_____ _____ _____

_____ _____ _____

_____ _____ _____

_____ _____ _____

Teaching Spelling So That Students Remember What They Have Learned

You want your students to care about correct spelling in all of their work, to learn to spell, and to remember what they learned. You want your students to take an active part in their learning. You are about to encounter a method of teaching spelling that research has proven to be extremely effective. It is called the **Test-Study-Test Method**, and it contributes significantly to students' learning how to spell in the short and long term. The basic principle is to have students correct their own spelling tests with the help of the teacher. This method has the following characteristics:

Students are given a test on the week's spelling words without any prior study. The teacher

* says the word.

* uses it in a sentence.

* says the word again.

* gives the student a signal to write the word.

Students correct their own papers.

* The teacher spells each word while it is written on the chalkboard or overhead.

* Students follow along and use a pencil to point to each letter written.

* Students circle spelling errors.

* Students write the correct spelling of missed words.

Students then study corrected words using the following specific set of procedures. The student

* says the word.

* hears the word.

* visualizes the word.

* writes the word.

* checks the spelling of his word with a correct model of the word.

Students then take another test using the same words.

* Students and teacher repeat the self-correcting and self-study steps.

Some Suggestions for Using the Test-Study-Test Method

Students need to know that the purpose of this process is to make them better spellers. The class ethos should consist of a positive view of the procedure. Initially, some students will be shocked to see how poorly they spell some of the words on the first test. They need to be reassured that the test is diagnostic and not meant for grading. To help students overcome any initial misgivings, some teachers explain that the spelling procedures will demonstrate how the process can help them. For example, some teachers will give a one- or two-word test with a long, unusual word like **axiomatic.** Following the process of self-correcting and retesting as stated above, most students easily learn to spell the new word, and then realize this particular process made it possible.

To encourage careful self-correcting, the teacher needs to look over the initial test to be sure that the self-correcting is proceeding properly.

To encourage self-correcting procedures and proper study activities, some teachers have found that close observation and student interviews are helpful.

Students are further motivated and involved when missed words are recorded on a personal spelling list and when weekly final test progress is recorded—perhaps in graph form or in a portfolio of final test papers. Graphs easily dramatize students' weekly progress.

Some teachers demonstrate and emphasize the study procedures. Surprising as it may sound, many students have no systematic way of studying their spelling-list words. Each step in the procedure is very important with particular attention given to the last two steps—writing and checking the word with a correct model. This is where students actually learn how much of the word they can spell and what needs to be done to fully master it. It is both motivating and rewarding once the whole word is spelled correctly.

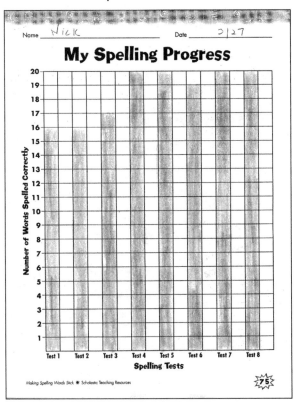

Promoting Spelling Achievement

Following are some practical suggestions supplied by researchers and teachers to promote student achievement in spelling:

 ✳ When a student asks how to spell a word, have the student try writing it and then compare it with a model either provided by the teacher or book.

 ✳ Teach the high-frequency words that students encounter in their writing.

* The **Test-Study-Test Method** is superior in comparison to writing each word five times.

* More time needs to be set aside for practice.

* Pointing out difficult parts in spelling a word is not effective in learning to spell.

* Students do better when they use an efficient study method.

* Students need to follow up on missed words.

* Students do better when they take responsibility for their progress.

* Teachers need to have a defined spelling instruction program.

* Students make greater progress when spelling is fun, interesting, and anxiety-free.

* Students' achievement increases when they see value in spelling.

* Teachers must address the needs of spellers at every skill level.

Notes